IDENTIFYING

TOY SOLDIERS

The new compact study guide and identifier

IDENTIFYING

TOY SOLDIERS

The new compact study guide and identifier

Norman Joplin

CHARTWELL
BOOKS, INC.

A QUINTET BOOK

Published by Chartwell Books
A Division of Book Sales, Inc.
114 Northfield Avenue
Edison, New Jersey 08837

This edition produced for sale
in the USA, its territories
and dependencies only.

ISBN 0-7858-0573-7

This book was designed and produced by
Quintet Publishing Limited
6 Blundell Street
London N7 9BH

Creative Director: Richard Dewing
Designer: James Lawrence
Project Editor: Alison Bravington
Editor: Tim Hall
Photographer: Ian Howes

The material in this publication previously
appeared in *Toy Soldiers* by Norman Joplin.

Typeset in Great Britain by
Central Southern Typesetters, Eastbourne
Manufactured in Hong Kong by
Regent Publishing Services Ltd
Printed in China by
Leefung-Asco Printers Ltd

CONTENTS

INTRODUCTION

T he practice of making miniature representations of soldiers can be traced back to Ancient Egyptian times, for the first small warrior-like figures were discovered in the tombs of the Pharoahs, where they were probably placed as part of religious ceremonies. Examples of Roman solid figures can be seen in the British Museum, London, and these are thought to have been playthings. The discovery at Xian in China of a full-size terracotta army bears testimony to the compulsion to reproduce real-life military soldiers.

Toy soldiers were for children. At first they were only available in limited numbers, and so were expensive and tended to be bought for the children of the

Austrian-made flat figures, c.1930, depicting soldiers of the American War of Independence. They are 30mm (1¼in) high.

nobility. Later, as manufacturing became more sophisticated, more soldiers at cheaper prices became available for all children to enjoy. By the late 19th century many a Victorian Christmas tree would be surrounded by all manner of toys, and for boys boxes of toy soldiers became a must.

The mid-18th century had seen the manufacture of some of the first commercial toy soldiers – flat, solid and made of lead – in Nuremberg in Germany. Heinrichsen was one of the major manufacturers. Semi-flat soldiers were also produced in Germany at this time. The toy soldier as we know it today probably evolved from the solid, fully rounded figures produced in France as early as 1790, and French and German companies were to dominate the market for another century. However, in 1893 William Britain, the son of a British toy manufacturer, invented the process of hollow-casting in lead and thereby initiated a toy-soldier revolution. Many UK firms imitated William Britain's methods, and the addition to their ranges of farms and zoos, boy scouts and cowboys and Indians, allowed these manufacturers to capture the lion's share of the British toy-soldier market.

Production continued throughout Europe up to and during World War I, with minor attempts being made to

A Nazi Sturmabteilung (stormtrooper) figure of the 1920s. It is 54mm (2¼in) high, and of unknown manufacture.

produce toy soldiers in the USA. By World War II the US market had become self-sufficient with ranges of slush- or hollow-cast toy soldiers, available through the "five and dime" stores. Later, these figures were given the nickname "dimestore"; the name has stuck and is now synonymous with US toy soldiers.

Most production stopped during World War II. Up to this time Germany, France and Italy had generally persisted with solid toy soldiers, while British makers continued to exploit the more economical method of hollow casting. However, in the mid-1930s some German companies had started producing composition figures, a combination of sawdust, pumice powder and glue, sculptured around a wire frame or armature. The majority of these German soldiers were troops of the Third Reich.

A hollow-cast British soldier in a World War I uniform. The UK manufacturer is unidentified, but the figure is 65mm (2½in) high and dates from around 1920.

After World War II the production of lead figures resumed, but experiments were already taking place with plastic, and by the early 1950s many UK and European companies were turning to the plastic injection moulding system. The manufacture of hollow-cast lead figures in the UK ceased in 1966 when legislation prohibited the sale of items which contained lead paint. Lead military miniatures of a "non-toxic" material (lead figures coated with a lead-free undercoat then painted with lead-free paint) filled the gap between 1966 and 1972, when white New Toy Soldiers were devised. The latter remain in production today.

As with all fields of collecting it is only when items become unusual or rare that the desire to accumulate either for pleasure or investment becomes paramount. So it is with toy soldiers. Collecting them started to become fashionable in the early 1960s as the hollow-cast and other lead soldiers were being discontinued. Some collectors are trying to relive the days of their childhood by acquiring the long-lost Christmas gifts of years gone by; others, perhaps from a military background, gain pleasure in forming parades or battlegrounds with toy soldiers. Whatever the reason, the hobby is now more for adults than children.

Plastic Wild West figures from Britain's Deetail range.

SOUVENIRS AND MEMORABILIA

A Scottish clansman, 100mm (4in) high, issued as a souvenir by Britains in the 1980s.

Toy soldiers sold as souvenirs in gift shops at airports, stately homes or tourist spots are becoming collectable. The Canadian market perhaps reflects this more than any other country. The military-style uniform of the Royal Canadian Mounted Police is recognized by all who are interested in soldiers, and toy-soldier manufacturers everywhere have capitalized on this by producing Mountie figures in all shapes, sizes and materials. Gift shops in the Niagara Falls area are crammed with examples of figures, fridge magnets and snow scenes.

West Point Academy in New York is also a popular spot, attracting thousands of visitors each year, and toy cadets are readily available. In Greece, toy versions of the famous Evzone or Royal Guard with their unusual, colourful uniforms are an attractive proposition. Scotland, whose tourist industry must be one of the world's largest, is well supplied with figures of Highlanders.

Toy shows also provide the collector with a chance to enhance a collection with souvenir badges or commemorative toy soldiers. This kind of merchandise is creating a new area of collecting, and sentimental collectors are now willing to pay inflated sums to acquire an item that celebrates a particular show.

The souvenir of a visit to Fort William Henry in Canada. The figure is 70mm (2¾in) high, and made by Minikins in Japan in 1950.

FOCUSING A COLLECTION

What soldiers you decide to collect is very much a matter of personal preference. However, there are some general factors which are useful to bear in mind before you get started as they will help you decide what direction you want your collection to go in and to make sure that you get maximum satisfaction from it.

The first question to ask yourself is what you are particularly interested in. Do you have a special area you want to focus on? Perhaps you will want to collect a certain type of soldier, or the work of a particular manufacturer. Collections can be arranged by manufacturer, size or type of material, or you can concentrate on certain periods in history, individual wars and campaigns, types of uniform – even particular regiments. It may be that at the beginning your collection will contain a mixture of items and as you become more involved you will decide how you want to specialize.

Another factor to bear in mind early on is cost. Some soldiers are much more expensive than others and you need to be able to assess which collecting areas you can afford. It is useful to scout around the various toy-soldier outlets if you are a newcomer to the hobby. This will give you an idea of what is available, and what the prices are, before you commit yourself to a purchase.

A solid-cast Highland officer, 54mm (2¼in) high, made around 1953 by the UK manufacturers Greenwood & Ball.

This kneeling rifleman, 75mm (3in) high, was made of composition material by Playwood Plastics in 1942.

WHERE TO BUY

Specialist collectors shops are found in most of the world's major cities. In addition to these, soldiers are commonly available from toy shows, flea markets, antique fairs and markets and at auctions.

Then there is always the chance that you will find something special at a car-boot sale, jumble sale or in a junk shop. Swapmeets are also popular, where you can meet other toy soldier enthusiasts and swap items.

LEFT *A US infantry figure manufactured during the early 1950s by Lincoln Logs.*

RIGHT *The American Soldier Co. made this Victorian-style sailor in a straw hat in the late 1920s.*

GUIDE TO AUCTION PROCEDURES

Auctions deserve a special mention. They are a good source of toy soldiers but can be daunting. Attending auctions can be both a source of revenue (if you are selling) or an opportunity to purchase. They also provide an opportunity to see what is on the market and what the prices are. There are three basic rules that will make the purchase of toy soldiers more enjoyable.

1. Make yourself aware of each individual auction-house's rules, commission rate and tax on commission.

2. If possible obtain a catalogue in advance and try to view the items you wish to purchase.

3. Consult the auction house regarding reserves for your items to ensure that if your property does not reach the expected price it will not be sold for less than your agreed reserve.

IDENTIFICATION OF TOY SOLDIERS

The majority of toy soldiers bear some mark on the underside of the base which is sometimes only the country of manufacture. Others have the name of the manufacturer or are marked in a way that gives an indication of its origin.

The British company, John Hill, marked "Johillco" or "John Hill" on their figures, but also stamped on an abbreviation of "copyright", spelt "copyrt". Britains marked nearly every figure, but used a variety of marks including their name, Britains Ltd. Only very early examples may not carry a mark. For a while the company used paper labels until all their moulds could be retooled to accommodate the copyright stamp. These paper labels are not always in place, which may be confusing for the novice collector.

Items found in their original boxes provide obvious evidence of the manufacturer. If you can get hold of original or reproduction catalogues this can also help with identification. There are a number of other books dealing with the subject of identification (see *Further Reading*, page 77) and the inexperienced collector will find these references very useful.

DISPLAYING YOUR COLLECTION

Part of the pleasure of having a collection of toy soldiers is being able to enjoy looking at them. The most popular method of displaying them is in cases or on shelves (it helps if these are enclosed so that dust does not become a problem, but air should be allowed to circulate round the items). The collector will decide which soldiers they want to display together, according to size, regiments and so on.

Some collectors prefer to arrange their figures so that they form a scene or diorama, perhaps depicting a real or imaginary reconstruction of a state occasion, battle or historical incident.

STORAGE AND CARE

Those unable to display their collections should ensure that lead soldiers are stored in a dry and well-ventilated area in strong cardboard boxes with a light covering of tissue paper. Plastic figures tend to become brittle and they should only be stored in a single row with no pressure being put on them.

A dimestore US GI of World War II vintage. The figure, 75mm (3in) high, was made by the American company, Barclay.

A perspex display box of Britains' figures, containing a Yeoman of the Guard, a Scots Guard and a Horse Guard together with a sentry box.

A word needs to be said about lead rot, sometimes called lead disease, which can appear in lead toy soldiers. Much inconclusive research has been carried out into its causes. It is possible that certain manufacturing methods may encourage lead rot, and it is known that storage in damp conditions does not help. It has also been proved that direct contact with oak wood can be a contributory factor. Display or storage in airtight conditions should be avoided.

The sign to watch out for is a grey powdering of the lead. As soon as you spot this, isolate the item from the others in your collection in case they also become affected.

REPAIR, RESTORATIONS AND CONVERSIONS

A growing number of collectors are trying to obtain broken or damaged toy soldiers, as their special interest is in restoring old toy soldiers to their former glory. Other people obtain broken or even complete toy soldiers and convert them into something else. They may put together pieces from two or more incomplete soldiers to make a whole one.

Doing this for your own pleasure is a very worthwhile exercise. However, it adds nothing to the value – it may even devalue an item – and most collectors look for figures that are in good condition.

VALUE

If a figure is in good condition when you buy it, and remains so, the likelihood is that its value will remain firm or will even increase with age. The value is also enhanced if the original packaging is intact, and collectors will pay a premium for soldiers still contained within their boxes.

For those who are interested in investment, it is a very good idea to keep an inventory of your collection. Make a note of the price you paid originally for each item and from time to time find out from dealers what it is currently worth. This means that you can keep a running total of the collection's value, which is useful insurance purposes and interesting.

USING THIS GUIDE

This book has been organized according to the materials from which the toy soldiers were made. Solid figures originated in a two-piece mould filled with molten lead; after cooling the figure was extracted. European manufacturers produced heads from separate moulds that were then plugged into the body. The hollow-cast method involved pouring molten lead into a cold mould, which had an air hole and an escape route for excess lead. The caster swirled the molten metal around the mould, with excess being poured through the hole. The figure – empty and light – was extracted from the mould with pliers. This process required about one-third of the amount of lead needed for solid figures. In the UK, government regulations governing the lead content of children's toys were introduced in 1966, and hollow-cast production effectively stopped.

Composition figures were generally made from a mixture of sawdust, glue, kaolin and casein, shaped around a wire armature, then dried and hand-painted. In the US toy soldiers were usually sold in stores that stocked numerous cheap items, the "five and dime" stores; hence the term "dimestore figures", devised by US collector Don Pielin. They were manufactured in a way similar to the hollow-cast figures, although the most accurate description would be slush-cast figures. Plastic figures are made by the process of injection moulding, in which the raw material is forced through holes in the centre of a brass mould by an injection machine. New Toy Soldiers are designed to look like hollow-cast figures, but are made of a non-toxic white metal alloy sculptured and produced from rubber moulds, by way of a centrifugal casting machine. Britain's New Metal Models, also designed to replace hollow-cast figures, require a metal die to facilitate the die-cast process. Aluminium figures were made in two halves from a sand-based moulding tray. Paper or cardboard figures generally stood on a wood-block base.

Throughout the book, the given heights refer to the toy soldiers, not the packaging. They are measured from the top of the base to the forehead, thus excluding bases and headgear. The British and European standard toy-soldier height is 54mm (2¼in), while the US standard is 70mm (2¾in).

SOLID FIGURES

In the late 18th century the French firm of Lucotte produced solid, fully rounded (ie not flat) toy soldiers depicting units of the French Army, at a height of 54mm (2¼in). These were the first figures intended to represent the real thing. By 1825 CBG Mignot of Paris had taken over Lucotte's, and began to introduce many new ranges of toy soldiers, hand-painted and fairly accurate in uniform detail. It is believed that Mignot went out of business in the early 1990s. Germany runs a close second to France in the production of solid-cast iron toy soldiers. Georg Heyde of Dresden produced toy soldiers from 1870 to 1944, when the factory was destroyed by Allied bombing raids. Heyde figures come in a range of sizes, but most are 45mm (1¾in) in height.

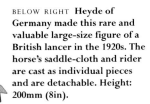

LEFT **A British soldier on a camel, a modern reproduction based on a 1930s design. Height: 60mm (2⅜in).**

BELOW LEFT **Two Roman figures from Mignot, probably issued during the 1970s from moulds made 60 years earlier. Height: 58mm (2⅛in).**

BELOW RIGHT **Heyde of Germany made this rare and valuable large-size figure of a British lancer in the 1920s. The horse's saddle-cloth and rider are cast as individual pieces and are detachable. Height: 200mm (8in).**

SOLID FIGURES

Like the French Mignot figures, Heyde toy soldiers have plug-in heads, which means that a whole variety of regiments could be created by putting different heads on different torsos. The Heyde range featured some massive display sets, including soldiers in action poses (firing, charging, etc.) and people in domestic poses (cooks, nurses, doctors and so on), together with additions like encampments of tents and field hospitals, which increased the play value for children. Mignot preferred to remain with conventional marching or ceremonial troops.

BELOW LEFT **Georg Heyde made this Austrian infantryman, advancing with fixed bayonet c.1930. Height: 54mm (2¼in).**

BELOW RIGHT **Treasure Chest, a US manufacturer, produces a range depicting the American Civil War, of which this wounded Confederate soldier is part. Height: 54mm (2¼in).**

SOLID FIGURES

Solid toy soldiers, made for adult collectors, were available after World War II from exclusive shops such as Hummel and Tradition in London. Known as "connoisseur figures", they were usually at the standard height of 54mm (2¼in), although larger ones were made, sometimes in kit form, ready for the collector to assemble and paint in precise detail.

Holger Eriksson, a Swedish designer, created the Authenticast range for collectors, manufactured in Ireland for the American company Comet. He also designed some 30mm (1¼in) troops for Swedish African Engineers, a company based in South Africa. Figur of Italy and Alymer of Spain made similar items which were available only in the European market.

ABOVE **Solid connoisseur figures designed by Holger Eriksson. The kneeling figure to the right is a Comet item while the others and the box are Authenticast. Height: 54mm (2¼in).**

RIGHT **A Vatican Guard figure manufactured by the Italian company Figur. These models have plug-in heads. Height: 60mm (2⅜in).**

FAR RIGHT **Tradition of London manufactured this solid-cast miniature of an officer from the Zulu War in 1970. Height: 54mm (2¼in).**

SOLID FIGURES

Between 1950 and 1970 Charles
Stadden and Rose Miniatures were two
of the best-known manufacturers of
connoisseur figures. The interest in
military miniatures was particularly
strong in Britain and France, where these
expensive items could be purchased in
shops near the Musée de l'Armée, and
in the United States.

BELOW **The US Honor Guard is
an unusual subject, here
portrayed by Stadden and sold
through the former London
Collector's Shop in the 1950s
and 1960s. Height: 54mm
(2¼in).**

ABOVE RIGHT **This British
officer of 1815 was made by
Russell Gamage to celebrate
the coronation of Queen
Elizabeth II. Height: 54mm
(2¼in).**

ABOVE LEFT **This intricately
painted figure of a soldier
reading orders was made by
Greenwood and Ball in the late
1960s. Height: 54mm (2¼in).**

LEFT **This volunteer of 1815,
made in 1973, is easily
identifiable as a Stadden
product by the thin, tinplate
base and the paper label
describing the soldier. Height:
54mm (2¼in).**

SOLID FIGURES

Connoisseur figures do not form a major part of the contemporary collecting scene, but they are historically interesting as the first miniature soldiers to be made specifically for adults. A fascinating development since the collapse of the USSR has been the arrival on the world market of Russian companies selling traditional solid-cast toy soldiers. The Anglo-Russian Toy Soldier Company and Insel are two such concerns; it remains to be seen whether their products will ever become collectors' items.

BELOW **These solid, rather crude figures were probably made in the USSR c.1968. Height: 52mm (2⅛in).**

ABOVE **Napoleon and his generals at a map table, made by Charles Stadden in the mid-1960s. Height: 30mm (1¼in).**

BELOW **Insel of Moscow made this hand-painted 1812 soldier and presented it to the author in 1993. Height: 60mm (2⅜in).**

HOLLOW-CAST FIGURES

In 1893 William Britain Jnr, the son of a UK toy manufacturer, conceived and perfected the hollow-cast method of making toy soldiers. It revolutionized the market, hitherto dominated by solid figures made in France and Germany.

The first hollow-cast figures were a set of mounted Life Guards, and so began a long line of issues depicting regiments of the British Army. Later, the scope widened to include foreign armies, such as in the Armies of the World series.

The Britain toy soldiers were an instant success with children, partly because they were cheaper and came packaged in attractive red boxes, and partly because they had movable arms.

ABOVE **The Bodyguard of the Emperor of Abyssinia, a Britains' Armies of the World set made prior to World War II. A valuable feature is that the soldiers are still tied into the box with thread. Height: 54mm (2¼in).**

RIGHT **Since the introduction in 1893 of the Life Guards, Britains has issued numerous updated versions of the regiment's uniforms. This one dates from the 1950s. Height: 90mm (3½in).**

HOLLOW-CAST FIGURES

Britains' success with hollow-cast figures brought it problems in the early 20th century. Smaller companies – A. Fry, C.D. Abel & Co., and Hanks Bros for example – sold flagrant, and sometimes cheaper, copies of Britains' products. This pirating only ceased when Britains successfully sued its rivals. From 1900 Britains applied copyright to its figures, indicated at first by means of a paper sticker on the underside of the soldier's base, and later by stamping the tradename, date and copyright mark on the base or bellies of cavalry horses. The paper stickers can help to date soldiers, and can also add to their value.

ABOVE **This Britains' cannon was used with hollow-cast US Civil War figures in the 1950s, as a Waterloo cannon in the 1960s, and with plastic Eyes Right and Herald soldiers until the early 1980s. Height: 54mm (2¼in).**

Both A. Fry and Hanks Bros did produce soldiers of their own designs. The khaki-clad Canadian soldier (LEFT) was sold by Fry as part of a series called Sons of the Empire. The guardsman at the trail (FAR LEFT) was made by Hanks Bros. Height: 54mm (2¼in).

HOLLOW-CAST FIGURES

Britains issued its first examples of khaki-uniformed troops in 1899, and established a Paris office in 1905 leading to the creation of many figures based on French units. Gun teams and ambulance wagons with troops dressed in World War I uniforms were added in 1916. The UK factory scaled down its production during this war but the French office continued its output of new figures, and many of them are now collectors' items.

After the war horse-drawn vehicles, cowboys and Indians, boy scouts and artillery pieces were introduced to the Britains' range, and existing models were continually updated.

ABOVE **British Army-style labels were used by Britains for its khaki troops. Height: 54mm (2¼in).**

RIGHT **Britains' matchstick-firing 4.7in naval gun remained in production from the early 1900s until the mid-1970s. This boxed example is highly valued by collectors. Height: 54mm (2¼in) Length: 23cm (9in).**

HOLLOW-CAST FIGURES

The UK production of toy soldiers was halted throughout World War II, but postwar government restrictions on the supply of lead meant only a slow return to normality. Britains was forced to delete certain lines, including many of its Balkan soldiers and some of its other European figures. The company campaigned for the relaxation of controls, and it was perhaps at this time that the first experiments in plastic production were undertaken. Britains was eventually permitted to bolster the ailing national economy by producing toy soldiers for the export market, in particular the United States. Domestic production only regained its pre-war strength in the late 1940s.

This Britains' self-propelled 155mm gun, of c.1955, mounted on a Centurion tank body, is seen here with its original corrugated cardboard box. Height: 100mm (4in) Length: 300mm (12in).

HOLLOW-CAST FIGURES

In the late 1940s and early 1950s many new items appeared in the Britains sales catalogues. A good number of older lines, especially those representing foreign regiments whose nations had disappeared during World War II, had been discontinued. The old Armies of the World series was replaced by Regiments of All Nations, containing foreign and British Commonwealth and Empire troops of the postwar period.

Picture Packs – single toy soldiers in individual boxes – were issued between 1959 and 1965. They were mainly taken from existing sets and packaged separately, although a few new figures were designed to increase the range. These are rare and much sought after by collectors.

ABOVE **A Regiments of All Nations box set. The blue slip of paper was a packer's reference, included to enable the customer to return damaged or unsatisfactory sets to Britains.**

LEFT **This mounted Life Guard dates from 1959, and was only available in Britains' Picture Pack series. Height: 90mm (3½in).**

HOLLOW-CAST FIGURES

In 1954, Roy Selwyn Smith (previously an employee of M. Zang, the manufacturer of Herald plastic soldiers) was employed by Britains as a designer. Amongst other things, he created for them a superb series of action figures entitled Knights of Agincourt. They were a welcome addition to the range of historical figures, and a departure from the somewhat rigid toy soldiers previously produced.

ABOVE **A Britains' box lid from c.1954. The Historical Series label was used for several different sets, including Coronation issues and Knights of Agincourt figures.**

BELOW **Britains' Knights of Agincourt boxed set, designed by Roy Selwyn Smith. Height: 54mm (2¼in).**

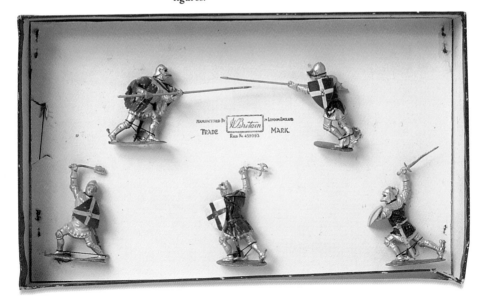

HOLLOW-CAST FIGURES

For many years John Hill & Co., sometimes known as Johillco, was second in size to Britains and Britains' main rival. George Wood, the company's founder, had been a Britains' employee and had learnt his hollow-casting skills there before striking out on his own in London in 1898. Wood did not imitate or copy Britains' figures. Rather he designed his own unique ranges, which are, some would say, on a par with Britains. John Hill figures appear more animated and reflect the kinds of positions that would actually be adopted by soldiers in battle. The company's success derived from this liveliness, which contrasted sharply with Britains' rigid marching or parade-order toy soldiers.

RIGHT **A John Hill & Co. mounted Royal Scots Grey standard bearer. The lead flag was replaced by a paper version when lead was in short supply after 1945. Height: 90mm (3½in).**

BELOW LEFT **An airman in a donkey jacket, made by John Hill & Co. and one of a range issued during the 1930s. Height: 54mm (2¼in).**

BELOW RIGHT **A John Hill & Co. Highland piper. This figure was available in many tartans and came in many grades of paint; the more intricate the tartan, the higher the price. Height: 90mm (3½in).**

BELOW CENTRE **A guardsman, kneeling and firing. This was a typical John Hill & Co. figure of the 1950s. Height: 54mm (2¼in).**

HOLLOW-CAST FIGURES

Right up until World War II John Hill & Co. continued to invest heavily in new ranges of toy soldiers. However, its London factory was bombed during the wartime Blitz. The moulds somehow survived and were bought and taken to Burnley in Lancashire, where a consortium of businessmen set up a new factory. Several new issues were designed in 1955, but the company failed to anticipate the demise of hollow-cast figures and did not invest in plastic injection moulding technology. Johillco was forced into liquidation during the early 1960s.

ABOVE This nurse figure was in production with John Hill & Co. both before and after World War II. Height: 54mm (2¼in).

ABOVE This khaki-clad charging figure was first made by John Hill & Co. in the early 1900s, and remained in production for many years in this form. Height: 90mm (3½in).

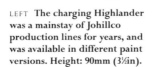

LEFT The charging Highlander was a mainstay of Johillco production lines for years, and was available in different paint versions. Height: 90mm (3½in).

ABOVE A John Hill & Co. mounted Field Marshal with baton, made during the 1950s. Height: 90mm (3½in).

27

HOLLOW-CAST FIGURES

In the years after 1893 over 100 UK firms were involved at one time or another in the production of hollow-cast toy soldiers and figures. Before 1914 A. Fry, Hanks Bros, BMC, Reka and John Hill & Co. were among William Britain's most prolific competitors, but the first three mentioned were out of business by 1939. Crescent bought out Reka in 1932 and continued to make lead figures until 1959, and both Charbens and Taylor & Barratt emerged in 1920. Many of these companies successfully converted to plastic production after World War II. A handful of new companies emerged after World War II, with Timpo (short for Toy Importers) being by far the most successful. Between 1946 and 1955, and with the assistance of Roy Selwyn Smith, it produced some of the best post-war hollow-cast toy soldiers.

LEFT **This Timpo knight was part of the King Arthur and the Knights of the Round Table set released to coincide with the MGM film. The plume is an airgun dart. Height: 54mm (2¼in).**

ABOVE RIGHT **Two soldiers from the Timpo US GI range of the early 1950s. The line included troops in both action and domestic poses. Height: 54mm (2¼in).**

RIGHT **A Red Indian, produced by Harvey in the UK c.1951. Height: 54mm (2¼in).**

LEFT **This splendid cowboy was produced by the Fylde Manufacturing Co. in 1951. John Hill & Co. took over Fylde and continued to produce this item. Height: 90mm (3½in).**

HOLLOW-CAST FIGURES

Britains' toy soldiers were more expensive than those of many other manufacturers, and were obtainable from Harrods and Hamleys in London and other up-market outlets. The figures produced by other UK companies such as Benbros, John Hill & Co., Crescent and Timpo were cheaper, and widely available from chain stores like Woolworths and independent high-street shops. European and American manufacturers did adopt the hollow-cast production method, but never to the same extent as British companies.

LEFT **This guardsman was one of many types made in vast numbers by Crescent in the 1950s. Height: 54mm (2¼in).**

BELOW LEFT **These two drummers are part of a cheap range of about 175 figures produced by Benbros in the early 1950s. Height: 54mm (2¼in).**

BELOW RIGHT **This French sailor was hollow-cast by GM in Paris in the mid-1950s. Height: 52mm (2¼in).**

HOLLOW-CAST FIGURES

Edward Jones of Chicago was one of the few US manufacturers to use hollow-casting methods, relying on the UK firm of Sale to supply moulds. Jones was a brilliant designer but a poor salesman, and his commercial ventures failed. Today his figures are much sought after.

LEFT **This Greek Evzone figure by Edward Jones is a rare piece. The Chicago Historical Society has a large display of items donated by Jones.**

BELOW **A rare, individually boxed example of a Royal Canadian Mounted Policeman produced by Crescent for the Canadian centennial in 1967. It is probably one of Crescent's last hollow-cast figures. Height: 90mm (3½in).**

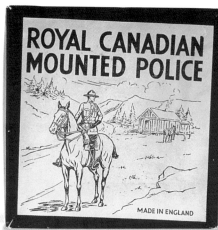

HOLLOW-CAST FIGURES

French manufacturers such as Mignot, LP and GM adopted hollow-cast methods with more enthusiasm than the Americans, but little research on these companies has been carried out. The subjects were mainly French troops from the Napoleonic era or action figures from World War I.

BELOW LEFT **A beturbanned Mameluke of the Napoleonic period, made by an unidentified French company. Height: 54mm (2¼in).**

ABOVE **An unusual French-made British Tommy throwing a grenade. Height: 54mm (2¼in).**

BELOW RIGHT **Two French-made figures of Napoleon's Imperial Guard, whose large heads give them a toy-like appearance. Height: 54mm (2¼in).**

COMPOSITION FIGURES

The most popular composition materials for making toy soldiers – sawdust, glue, kaolin and cassein` – were first combined in Vienna in 1898 by a company called Pfeiffer. The compound was particularly common in Germany, and in 1926 the Hausser brothers of Stuttgart adopted the name Elastolin for their composition figures, a name now widely used to describe all such items. Elastolin produced mostly 70mm (2¾in) figures from 1904 to 1943, although sizes did vary and could be as large as 100mm (4in). Most of the world's armed forces were portrayed in the range during the 1920s, but the rise of Nazism in the 1930s led to an emphasis on the German armed forces.

ABOVE **German bandsmen, typical of the mid-1930s. The oval bases are characteristic of Hausser-Elastolin figures. Height: 65mm (2½in).**

LEFT **Two Elastolin figures: a guardsman at slope arms, and an officer carrying a sword. Height: 100mm (4in).**

COMPOSITION FIGURES

Apart from Germany few countries used composition for toy soldiers. As a stopgap measure while lead was in short supply after World War II, the Brent Toy Co issued a small range of khaki-clad infantry in the UK, based on

Elastolin and using the name Elastolene. For the same reason, Timpo introduced some small Timpolene figures to its UK range. Toydell was another UK manufacturer to produce composition or plaster soldiers.

A nurse, probably made by a German or Austrian company in the 1930s. Height: 65mm (2½in).

Toydell made this Yeoman of the Guard as part of its gift range during the early 1950s. Height: 100mm (4in).

This British infantryman, of unknown manufacture, was sold through Kresge stores in the US for a short period after World War II. Height: 60mm (2⅜in).

COMPOSITION FIGURES

During the late 1940s, again in the struggle to avoid the problems of lead shortage, the British firm Riviere & Willett issued some large-size composition models, more akin to statuettes, and in the 1950s the Miller company in the USA made some plaster-of-Paris figures. Available in "five and dime" stores, these figures are prone to chipping and are collected by a minority of American enthusiasts.

RIGHT **Miller plaster figures, depicting a stretcher party and a field hospital nurse. Height: 100mm (4in).**

FAR LEFT **A World War I standard-bearing French soldier made by an unknown French company. Height: 70mm (2¾in).**

LEFT **Although this Indian Army Sikh of c.1938 is more ornamental than toy-like, it was sold as a toy soldier. It was made of plaster in the UK. Height: 100mm (4in).**

DIMESTORE FIGURES

Barclay was founded in 1924 by the brothers Donze and Michael Levy, in West Hoboken, New Jersey. It became the USA's largest manufacturer of toy soldiers and figures, with the factory later moving to Union City and West New York.

The nucleus of the company's production was devoted to models of US armed forces, mostly in action, and Wild West figures. Many other ranges were introduced over the years. The pre-1939 khaki troops had removable tin helmets, while post-war figures had fixed helmets. After 1945 the figures' expensive lead bases were removed and the feet widened, giving rise to the name of "podfoot figures". Many were built to a standard size of 70mm (2¾in), but some were made at 45mm (1¾in) and others at 75mm (3in). Barclay ceased trading in 1971.

Barclay World War I grenade thrower, made in 1935.
Height: 75mm (3in).

BELOW LEFT A Barclay-made podfoot soldier of the 1950s. The red uniform is scarce, and the figure is thought to represent enemy troops from the Korean War.
Height: 75mm (3in).

This searchlight operator was cast as one piece by Barclay, and was issued with minor variations seven times.
Height: 75mm (3in).

BELOW RIGHT Barclay's kneeling nurse is similar in design to the Elastolin nurses made in Germany.
Height: 75mm (3in).

DIMESTORE FIGURES

Maurice and Jack Manoil joined with Walter Baetz in 1924 to form the company that bears their name. It produced soldiers that were similar in scale and style to those made by Barclay, but with perhaps just an ounce more character than the latter's. The Manoil Happy Farm civilian range was produced to reflect US social history and, like Barclay, the company produced a wide range of military vehicles.

BELOW LEFT **An intricately made Manoil dimestore anti-aircraft gun and gunner. Height: 75mm (3in).**

ABOVE **This fine Manoil parachutist fully reveals the company's skilful design techniques. Height: 75mm (3in).**

BELOW RIGHT **A naval ensign from the Manoil range. Height: 75mm (3in).**

DIMESTORE FIGURES

Grey Iron, another manufacturer of dimestore figures, used a cast-iron process (which seems to have increased paint loss from the figures) and adopted the Barclay size and style for its toy soldiers, as did Tommy Toy, All Nu and the Japanese-made Minikins. Other notable US makers, such as the American Soldier Co., McLoughlin, Lincoln Logs and Warren made figures of a size similar to the UK standard of 54mm (2¼in).

BELOW LEFT **Grey Iron made this seated machine gunner in the 1930s. Height: 75mm (3in).**

ABOVE **US volunteers made by the American Soldier Co. (tradename Eureka) in 1906. Height: 54mm (2¼in).**

BELOW CENTRE AND RIGHT **The Mountie was part of a series of cowboys and Indians made by Lincoln Logs, while the sailor is from the company's standard military range. Height: 52mm (2⅛in).**

DIMESTORE FIGURES

In the USA, during the 1930s, toy soldiers were frequently made at home. Home-casting sets, easily available by mail order, and containing metal moulds, a bar of lead, a ladle and a melting pot, became very popular. The subjects were mainly US figures. Sachs was perhaps the best-known manufacturer along with Henry Schierke. In the mid-1980s Ron Eccles of Burlington, Iowa, acquired many of Barclay's and Manoil's original moulds and began to produce excellent copies of the famous dimestore soldiers. Ron's wife, Debbie, catalogues the products and paints the items in a style that evokes the charm and character of the originals. Each item is marked "Eccles Brothers" with the current date.

Playwood Plastics made this composition soldier wearing a gas mask and holding a flare gun. Height: 75mm (3in).

Soldiers in domestic poses were frequently included in dimestore ranges, and this "correspondent" figure is a good example. Height: 75mm (3in).

Nurse with an ether bottle and mask, manufactured by Eccles Brothers as a modern casting from an old mould. Height: 65mm (2½in).

DIMESTORE FIGURES

Japanese-made toy soldiers were also sold through dimestores, and can therefore be classified as dimestore figures. After World War II a number of US companies imported lead, composition and celluloid toy soldiers from Japan, many of which were copies of US or European products. The quality varied: Minikins made high-quality lead figures, while Trico made crude composition versions. Nevertheless, all sold in vast numbers and have a strong following among today's collectors. Particularly valuable are items in boxes marked "Occupied Japan".

This Japanese-made Indian probably dates from the 1930s. It has a pivot through the body so that both arms can move, a very unusual feature. Height: 54mm (2¼in).

The solid figure of this West Point cadet was made in occupied Japan just after World War II, probably as a souvenir item. Height: 54mm (2¼in).

This dimestore flat figure, made in 1952, was probably intended as a Christmas novelty item. Height: 70mm (2¾in).

PLASTIC FIGURES

The first viable plastic toy soldiers date from the late 1940s. It is uncertain which manufacturer can claim to be first in the field, but in the US Beton was supplying dimestores with unpainted 60mm (2⅜in) figures of GIs just after World War II. In the UK Airfix offered plastic soldiers and cowboys and Indians for sale in 1947. Around this same time Malleable Mouldings of Deal in Kent imported from Eire a range of sophisticated plastic figures designed by Holger Eriksson. The venture failed, probably because it was ahead of its time.

ABOVE These self-coloured American infantry figures, made in the late 1940s by Beton, were sold through dimestores, and Woolworths in Britain. Height: 60mm (2⅜in).

LEFT Two examples of 1940s figures – a mounted Roundhead and a guardsman at the slope – from the pioneering but ill-fated Malleable Mouldings. Height: 90mm (3½in) and 54mm (2¼in).

PLASTIC FIGURES

In the 1950s some UK hollow-cast manufacturers – such as Timpo, Cherilea and Crescent – converted their existing moulds to fit plastic injection moulding machines. However, the first UK maker to issue plastic figures was Zang Products (later Herald) of east London. Zang employed a number of designers in the early 1950s, and the factory produced some of the finest plastic toy soldiers ever made.

ABOVE This King Arthur figure from Timpo has a good-quality paint finish, and was part of a series issued in the mid-1960s. Height: 54mm (2¼in).

BELOW Trojan warriors from Zang's Herald range of the early 1950s. Height: 54mm (2¼in).

RIGHT Two Highland soldiers from the Herald range. Height: 54mm (2¼in).

PLASTIC FIGURES

In the early 1950s Zang introduced a large number of new plastic figures, including khaki battledress infantry, American Civil War soldiers, Foot Guards, Life Guards, Horse Guards, Highlanders, and cowboys and Indians. They came packed in colourful boxes or on display cards of four figures, and quickly became popular with children. In 1953 the tradename Herald was adopted, and a herald logo was embossed on the underside of each figure's base.

ABOVE **A British officer and sentry from the Herald range of British Army khaki troops. Height: 54mm (2¼in).**

BELOW **Four Herald figures: two mounted Household Cavalry troopers and two dismounted. Height: 90mm (3½in) and 54mm (2¼in).**

PLASTIC FIGURES

In the mid-1950s Wm Britain Ltd took over the Herald name and company. The name survived until the early 1980s as the Britains' tradename for the bulk of its plastic figures. Ironically, in 1957 lead copies of plastic Herald figures began to be exported from Hong Kong to the UK and USA!

In the late 1950s Britains revolutionized the world of plastic figures with the introduction of the Swoppet range. All the pieces in the range, including individual pistols, were removable and interchangeable, and so could be "swopped" with other figures.

LEFT A cowboy, seated on a barrel, from Britains' Swoppet range. Height: 54mm (2¼in).

BELOW LEFT In 1955 AHI of Hong Kong made this hollow-cast lead copy of a plastic Herald American Civil War infantryman. Height: 54mm (2¼in).

BELOW RIGHT A cowboy and Indian from Britains' Herald range. This series also included mounted figures. Height: 45mm (1¾in).

PLASTIC FIGURES

In 1960 Britains introduced the Eyes Right range to fill the gap caused by the disappearance of many hollow-cast ceremonial or full-dress types of toy soldier. The range carried some Swoppet-style features, since the heads and arms were movable, and it began with Guards figures, Royal Marines and other British regiments. US Marines and US Army bands were later included. The final Eyes Right figures, the Bahamas Police and Royal Canadian Mounted Police, appeared in 1962.

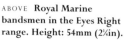

BELOW LEFT **Two soldiers of the Scots Guards in the Britains' Eyes Right range. Height: 54mm (2¼in).**

ABOVE **Royal Marine bandsmen in the Eyes Right range. Height: 54mm (2¼in).**

BELOW RIGHT **A piper of the Scots Guards. Note the paper banner on the bagpipes of this Eyes Right figure. Height: 54mm (2¼in).**

PLASTIC FIGURES

Foot soldiers of the American Civil War had formed part of the Herald range from the early 1950s, but it took some 10 years for Swoppet-type mounted troops to join them. The old foot figures were phased out and replaced by a newly designed set. Most of the other ranges were extended, with siege weapons being added in 1967 to enhance the Swoppet range of knights.

ABOVE **American Civil War figures: examples of both the old fixed-limb Herald infantry figures and the Swoppet-style movable-limb figures. Height: 90mm (3½in) and 54mm (2¼in).**

RIGHT **Swoppet-style movable-limb figures from a set reintroduced by Britains to celebrate the American Bicentennial in 1976. Height: 54mm (2¼in).**

45

PLASTIC FIGURES

In 1971 Britains introduced the Deetail range of plastic fixed-limb figures mounted on metal bases. Although it was aimed at the children's market, it is now a popular area for adult collectors. It consisted initially of US and German infantrymen of World War II vintage. In 1972 the production of Herald plastic figures was finally sub-contracted to a Hong Kong company, on the grounds of cost.

BELOW **A Britains' Deetail Land-Rover, complete with gun. Height (of figures): 54mm (2¼in).**

ABOVE **Two medieval archers from Britains' Herald range, manufactured in Hong Kong. Height: 54mm (2¼in) and 45mm (1¾in).**

BELOW RIGHT **US infantrymen and recoil-less rifle, from the Deetail range. Height: 54mm (2¼in).**

PLASTIC FIGURES

Britains' Deetail range expanded immensely after 1971 to include Japanese soldiers, British 8th Army personnel, the German Afrika Korps, French Foreign Legionnaires, Napoleonic troops, and Arab and Mexican warriors. In the 1980s Turks and medieval knights were added, as were several series of spacemen. However, as the importance of Britains' New Metal Models has grown, the range of plastic figures has diminished. The most recent Deetail figures are the Knights of the Sword.

TOP **Motorized infantry and rifleman of the German army, from Britains' Deetail range. Height (of figures): 54mm (2¼in).**

ABOVE **Three Deetail figures: two British khaki-clad soldiers, and a Japanese infantryman. Height: 54mm (2¼in).**

BELOW **A Deetail battle scene: Arabs attacking soldiers of the French Foreign Legion. Height: 54mm (2¼in).**

PLASTIC FIGURES

The late 1950s saw many UK manufacturers take on the challenge of the Swoppet-style plastic toy soldiers, so successfully pioneered by Britains. Timpo adopted a similar system and went on to produce hundreds of different figures from its factory in Shotts,

Lanarkshire. Norman Tooth, a remarkable Timpo designer, continued to come up with new ideas, and in the late 1970s devised a remarkable machine that could convert, cut, paint and assemble a complete figure. This automatic process produced Timpo's

last range in 1978, a series of Vikings, mounted and on foot, but unfortunately the company ceased production in 1979.

ABOVE RIGHT **This Timpo mounted Viking was one of the last pieces to be made by Norman Tooth's automatic process. The figure has a movable head and waist. Height: 90mm (3½in).**

ABOVE LEFT **Knights of the Helm was an attempt by Timpo to inject more detail – such as the ornate head-dress – into its Swoppet-style figures. Height: 54mm (2¼in).**

LEFT **A Timpo mounted cowboy of the 1970s. Note the fringed Cheyenne-type jacket. It also has a movable head and waist. Height: 54mm (2¼in).**

PLASTIC FIGURES

The UK boom in the production of plastic toy soldiers lasted roughly from 1955 to 1980. Cherilea, whose figures were 60mm (2⅜in) high, introduced many new ranges, including even a Tudor execution set. Charbens covered many familiar subject areas, as well as the less-common pirates, Cossacks and a bull-fighting set. Crescent introduced a superb series of British World War I troops, and also produced knights and Robin Hood, cowboys and Indians, which were eventually obtainable in cereal packets.

ABOVE RIGHT **This Mexican bandit with a money pouch was part of an animated Wild West set made by Crescent. Height: 60mm (2⅜in).**

ABOVE LEFT **This plastic Saracen with a spear was previously made by Charbens in lead from a hollow-cast mould. Height: 50mm (2in).**

FAR LEFT **A plastic World War I grenade thrower, part of a series of nine figures manufactured by Crescent in the 1960s. Height: 56mm (2¼in).**

LEFT **Cherilea made this unusual Chinese infantryman with a flamethrower in the 1960s, as part of a series of six. Height: 60mm (2⅜in).**

PLASTIC FIGURES

John Hill & Co., the UK's second-largest producer of hollow-cast figures, made little effort in the 1950s to change to plastic materials. It converted some hollow-cast moulds, but it never invested in injection moulding equipment, believing that plastic would only be a short-lived phenomenon. It even turned down the chance to supply Kelloggs with hundreds of thousands of plastic figures for cereal packets. By the early 1960s John Hill & Co. was out of business.

LEFT **This clansman, issued under John Hill & Co's Monarch label in the late 1950s, is from one of the company's few plastic sets. Height: 54mm (2⅛in).**

BELOW **Poplar Playthings, a Welsh company, made this Roman chariot and charioteer in the mid-1950s. Although classed as plastic by collectors, the figures are actually made of rubber. Height: 80mm (3⅛in).**

PLASTIC FIGURES

By 1980 most UK plastic-soldier manufacturers had gone out of business, leaving only Cavendish Miniatures of Windsor, Airfix and Britains in production. Cavendish continues to make plastic figures (having begun in the early 1950s) and acts as a wholesaler to the trade. It also specializes in souvenir items made of solid lead.

In 1989 Giles Brown of Dorset Soldiers bought many of the old Cherilea plastic moulds and started to reissue self-coloured figures at an affordable price. In 1990 Marlborough of Wales launched a similar operation when it purchased the redundant Charbens' moulds, and Toyway now reissues the Timpo range.

ABOVE **This Tudor-style swordsman was a 1990s reissue by Dorset Soldiers from the Cherilea original mould. Height: 60mm (2⅜in).**

ABOVE **Many companies copied the plastic Herald soldiers. This example was made by VP, a small British firm. Height: 54mm (2¼in).**

BELOW **This box of 1750 infantry is one of Cavendish Miniature's early sets, and forms part of a range issued continuously since 1958. Height: 54mm (2¼in).**

BRITISH REGIMENTS 1751

Grenadier, 1st FOOT GUARDS   "Royal" Drummer   Officer, 59th Foot   Grenadier, 59th FOOT

PLASTIC FIGURES

The US market for plastic toy soldiers was dominated by Louis Marx & Co. This famous company specialized in the production of large boxed display sets, known as playsets, which included not only unpainted toy soldiers – sometimes over 100 figures – but also buildings and accessories. Painted Marx soldiers were available in the Warriors of the World series, and over the years the company covered most major historical periods and wars. Marx also issued 150mm (6in) figures, and used both hard and soft plastics. There were Marx factories in Germany, Hong Kong and Wales. Marx items are avidly collected, and the market even supports a specialist magazine. Michael Ellis's London-based company, Marksmen, has carved out a lucrative business in the reissue of original Marx figures.

ABOVE **Modern reproductions by Marksmen of an original Marx set. Height: 60mm (2⅜in).**

BELOW LEFT **This large 150mm (6in) unpainted figure of a World War II GI was made by Marx.**

BELOW RIGHT **This Robin Hood figure was a popular Marx item in the 1960s. They were available painted or unpainted in self-coloured plastic, with the character's name embossed in the base. Height: 60mm (2⅜in).**

PLASTIC FIGURES

Apart from the UK, the US and Hong Kong, European manufacturers were the other major producer of plastic soldiers. Starlux of France used hard plastic to depict a wide range of Napoleonic troops, Foreign Legionnaires and military cadets. The figures were realistically modelled in good action poses with a highly detailed paint finish, and at its peak Starlux covered many other subjects. It also issued a second-grade series of cheaper and less-detailed toy soldiers, slightly smaller than 54mm (2¼in).

Three Starlux figures: the female Russian soldier (BELOW LEFT) is an unusual subject; the medieval court jester (LEFT) is from the first-grade range, while the paratrooper (BELOW RIGHT) is a smaller second-grade figure. Height: 54mm (2¼in).

PLASTIC FIGURES

Spain's main producer of toy soldiers was Reamsa, whose range included many figures from the Spanish armed forces as well as medieval characters and Moors. Popular from the 1950s until the 1970s, Reamsa toy soldiers are now being reissued by an enterprising collector, Ric Bracamontes of the Chicago-based Company B. Reamsa itself stopped trading in the late 1970s.

A rare plastic figure of a toytown soldier at port arms, made by Quiralux of France. The series moulds were sold in the early 1950s to Wend-Al in the UK, which converted them to make "unbreakable" aluminium figures. Height: 52mm (2⅛in).

This Spanish Army standard bearer is one of a set of 20 Reamsa pieces. Height: 60mm (2⅜in).

PLASTIC FIGURES

After World War II Hausser, the German company famous for its pre-war composition Elastolin figures, turned to the production of plastic toy soldiers. It introduced a series of large-scale Romans, knights and cowboys and Indians, based on some of its pre-war designs. Later it released figures based on World War II German troops. Hausser eventually went out of business in the late 1970s, a victim of the fashion for high-tech toys. Gaugemaster, a UK company, has recently tried to revive the Hausser plastic range, but with limited success.

BELOW **Trooper of the Royal Canadian Mounted Police, made by Hausser for the souvenir market. Height: 65mm (2½in).**

ABOVE **This splendid Roman cavalryman was one of a series released by Hausser in the 1960s and 1970s. Height: 100mm (4in).**

BELOW RIGHT **Mounted German officer. Hausser designed the figure to be removed from the horse. Height: 100mm (4in).**

PLASTIC FIGURES

Plastic toy soldiers made in Hong Kong flooded the world market for many years. These were usually unpainted, and although they were sometimes well detailed they are always classified by collectors as second grade. Furthermore, such figures were almost without exception pirated copies of US and European designs.

A Hong Kong copy of a Swoppet-style cowboy, with a movable waist and head. Height: 52mm (2⅛in).

This US infantryman in grey plastic is a typical Hong Kong product. Height: 80mm (3¼in).

NEW TOY SOLDIERS

In 1966 it became illegal in the UK to manufacture lead toy soldiers, thus leaving a gap in the market. Frank and Jan Scroby of London had been dealers in the old hollow-cast figures, but as they became increasingly scarce the Scrobys experimented with producing their own replacements. By 1973 they had successfully developed the Blenheim range of figures made from a non-toxic white metal alloy. These New Toy Soldiers, as they became known, were designed to sit alongside traditional hollow-cast items.

The Blenheim Highlander at the slope (LEFT) "steps" off on the opposite foot to most toy soldiers. The Zulu and his British enemy (BELOW) are animated pieces and something of a departure from Blenheim's standard marching figures. Height: 54mm (2¼in).

NEW TOY SOLDIERS

Blenheim's miniature masterpieces were an instant success with collectors. Shamus Wade, a long-established toy-soldier dealer, commissioned the Scrobys to produce the exclusive Nostalgia range of New Toy Soldiers for his mail-order business. The sets and individual figures depicted regiments of the British Commonwealth. During its latter years, as Blenheim itself grew bigger, the Nostalgia range was taken over by Peter Cowan and Andrew Rose.

BELOW **Blenheim box set by Frank and Jan Scroby. These blue boxes had gold inserts with slots for each figure. Height (of figures): 54mm (2¼in).**

ABOVE **This Chelsea Pensioner by Blenheim fits in well with military figures. Height: 54mm (2¼in).**

ABOVE **A Chinese soldier from the Boxer Rebellion, made by Blenheim for a well-known collector in the 1970s. Height: 54mm (2¼in).**

NEW TOY SOLDIERS

The Blenheim range was discontinued in 1982 after financial difficulties, but the Scrobys introduced the new Marlborough range later that year, to be sold at first through a US agent, Star Collectibles. A magnificent series, based on the Delhi Durbar of 1902, was released as well, devised so that the collector could add to the set over a period and ultimately build a complete Durbar. Sadly, the Marlborough range fell victim to economic recession in the mid-1990s, and production has stopped. Andrew Rose is another talented designer of New Toy Soldiers, and currently produces his own lines of Bastion and Wessex figures.

ABOVE **Two British figures in tropical-service dress, from Andrew Rose's Bastion range. Height: 54mm (2¼in).**

BELOW **A Marlborough box set by Frank and Jan Scroby. These boxes had foam inserts and sections in which each figure lay. Height (of figures): 54mm (2¼in).**

NEW TOY SOLDIERS

The Scrobys' successful ventures inspired many others to produce their own ranges of New Toy Soldiers. Typical of these was Mark Time of Croydon, London, which manufactured figures in the mid-1970s, and Charles Hall of Edinburgh, who will work to commissions. Thelma and Jack Duke of Ducal in Hampshire specialize in the making of ceremonial troops that depict many state occasions, such as the Trooping the Colour.

ABOVE **This Household Cavalry drum horse with its attractive box is characteristic of the high-quality work produced by Ducal. Height: 90mm (3½in).**

FAR LEFT **An unusual volunteer cyclist, from the Mark Time range. Height: 54mm (2¼in).**

LEFT **Adolf Hitler, portrayed by Charles Hall. Height: 70mm (2¾in).**

NEW TOY SOLDIERS

Another major New Toy Soldier company is Trophy Miniatures of Wales, run by Len Taylor. It has become world-famous for the quality of its designs and painting. The Zulu War features heavily in the Trophy range, and information on new designs and subject areas is available from the Guards Toy Soldier Centre at Wellington Barracks in London.

Trophy made this superb two-piece set of Winston Churchill mounted and firing a pistol at an attacking Dervisher. Height: 90mm (3½in) and 54mm (2¼in).

BELOW **Three early figures from Trophy Miniatures: a Royal Marine, a soldier of the West India Regiment, and an Indian Army officer. Height: 54mm (2¼in).**

NEW TOY SOLDIERS

In 1977 John Tunstill, the proprietor of Soldiers shop in Lambeth, London launched his own range, Soldiers Soldiers. The figures were partly designed by Andrew Rose, and although no longer in production, items are still available from existing stocks. Dorset Soldiers, owned by Giles Brown in Wiltshire, started the production of New Toy Soldiers in 1979 and has gone from strength to strength. A wide range of UK and foreign regiments are obtainable (as well as reissues of the old Cherilea plastic soldiers), and fresh additions are regularly announced via a catalogue.

BELOW **An inventive set from Dorset Soldiers, made of hand-painted white metal and designed to be used with the 54mm (2¼in) New Toy Soldiers.**

ABOVE **This Lancer officer was one of Trophy's earliest items, c.1974. The figure's oval base was discontinued soon afterwards. Height: 54mm (2¼in).**

ABOVE **A solid Bethnal Green volunteer, manufactured by John Tunstill in the 1970s as an exclusive souvenir of the Bethnal Green Museum of Childhood in London. Height: 54mm (2¼in).**

NEW TOY SOLDIERS

In recent years, the British Toy Soldier and Figure Show – Europe's largest toy-soldier event – has been attracting increasing numbers of exhibitors from the ranks of UK New Toy Soldier manufacturers. Many of these participants are private individuals, who do it purely for pleasure, such as Major Gavin Thompson of the Royal Military Police. Others, like Martin Tabony, treat the business as a cottage industry, while some are full-time professional manufacturers.

LEFT **A Royal Military Policeman, manufactured by Major Gavin Thompson under the name of Kidogo. Height: 54mm (2¼in).**

BELOW **"The Home Coming", an attractive set designed, sculpted and painted by Martin Tabony. Height: 54mm (2¼in).**

NEW TOY SOLDIERS

There are several reasons for the success of the New Toy Soldier phenomenon. Amongst them must be the careful attention to historical and period detail displayed by the best manufacturers (such as Steadfast Soldiers), high-quality craftsmanship, attractive packaging of the product and a thorough understanding of how to reach and appeal to the specialist collectors.

An attractive set of the Black Watch, complete with maxim gun and officer, produced by Steadfast Soldiers. Height: 54mm (2¼in).

NEW TOY SOLDIERS

There are several American producers of New Toy Soldiers, such as Somerset, Bill Hocker, Edward Burley, Joe Shimek, Stephen Dietz and Ron Wall. Perhaps the most successful is Bill Hocker of Berkeley, California. His commitment, eye for detail and exquisite design, and manufacturing techniques has ensured a worldwide reputation. Luigi and Monica Toiati of Rome fly the flag in Italy, under the tradename of Garibaldi.

RIGHT **Highland piper of the '45, made by Garibaldi of Italy. Height: 54mm (2¼in).**

BELOW **This set of a naval band from Bill Hocker has been shrink-wrapped so that collectors can display it without removing the figures. Height: 54mm (2¼in).**

RIGHT **A Red Indian brave, complete with removable lance, from Ron Wall of St Louis, Missouri. Height: 54mm (2¼in).**

NEW METAL MODELS

In 1973 Britains introduced its New Metal Models. Although this was the same year that the Scrobys launched the Blenheim range of similar-sounding New Toy Soldiers, in fact the two manufacturing processes are quite different from each other (see page 14 for further details). The first New Metal Model was a Scots Guard marching figure. After a slow start, Britains has recaptured a large slice of the international toy-soldier market, frequently by means of boxed sets in both limited and unlimited editions. The former were introduced in 1983, and their value to collectors obviously varies according to the number of sets issued.

ABOVE **A Britains' mounted trooper of the Life Guards. Height: 90mm (3½in).**

BELOW **The 2nd Life Guards in a Britains' boxed set of 1994. Height: 90mm (3½in).**

NEW METAL MODELS

Special Britains' issues, not included in the normal catalogue range, are sometimes available. For example, a 1984 exhibition, entitled "On Guard", and held at the London Toy and Model Museum prompted Britains to release two Argyll & Sutherland figures, packed on an open-fronted card and available only for the exhibition's duration. Both are now quite rare. 1985 saw the launch of a campaign to boost sales in Canada, including the issue of Mountie figures as part of the strategy.

BELOW **Two Britains' Argyll & Sutherland Highlanders from the 1984 London Toy and Model Museum exhibition. Height: 54mm (2¼in).**

ABOVE **A New Metal Model of a Royal Canadian Mounted Policeman. Height: 90mm (3½in).**

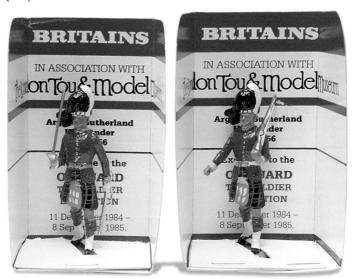

NEW METAL MODELS

Throughout the 1980s Britains continued to develop the use of boxed sets and limited editions as marketing tools. For example, in 1986 the Welsh Guards became available in a limited edition of 5,000, and to enhance US sales three sets of US Marine Corps figures were released. In 1987 this particular theme was developed with the inclusion of US Marine Corps bandsmen in the William Britain Collection. The same year also saw a Bahamas Police Band in a 5,000 limited-edition set; the same subject had previously been produced in hollow-cast form.

RIGHT **The Bahamas Police Band in Britains' 1987 edition, complete with certificate. Height: 54mm (2¼in).**

BELOW **Drummers and buglers of the US Marine Corps, displayed in Britains' perspex presentation box. Height: 54mm (2¼in).**

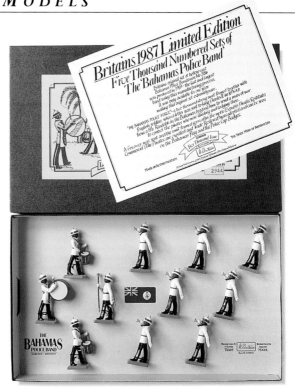

NEW METAL MODELS

The quality of Britains' New Metal Models received prestigious acclaim when two famous London stores, Harrods and Hamleys, both commissioned Britains to supply them with customized presentation boxes of soldiers. The Harrods' London Set contained a selection of the troops found performing ceremonial duties in the capital, together with a figure of the Queen mounted for Trooping the Colour. Both of these sets will undoubtedly increase in value. The production of other boxed sets continued to expand: amongst them in 1991, for example, were the 17th and 21st Lancers, together with the Irish Guards and the Somerset Light Infantry.

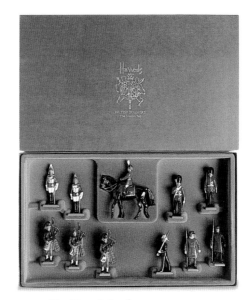

BELOW **A handsome Britains' set of The Duke of Cambridge's Own 17th Lancers. Height: 90mm (3½in).**

ABOVE **The Harrods London Set, commissioned from Britains by the famous store. Height: 54mm (2¼in).**

NEW METAL MODELS

In the 1990s Britains reverted to more traditional packaging methods: the famous red boxes with illustrated descriptive labels were reintroduced, and the company consciously emphasized the links between its New Metal Models and the old hollow-cast figures. In 1992 five new sets in red boxes were released, including the Royal Marine Light Infantry and the Middlesex Yeomanry. The same year also saw the issue of small boxes holding either one mounted or two foot figures, similar to the hollow-cast Picture Pack series. One such was a 1,000-box edition of a piper from the King's Own Scottish Borderers, produced for the British Association of Toy Retailers in time for the 1993 Britains' centenary celebrations.

ABOVE **A piper of the King's Own Scottish Borderers, released for the Britains' centenary. Height: 54mm (2¼in).**

BELOW **The Royal Marine Light Infantry, in a Britains' special collectors' edition. Height: 54mm (2¼in).**

NEW METAL MODELS

In 1992 Britains introduced another style of packaging, the "Grey Boxes" as they have become known. They were designed to feature a number of famous regiments, with each box containing ten figures. The toy soldiers fitted into slots, which enabled them to be lifted out and replaced in the groove of the box. Unfortunately, the venture was short-lived. For the company's centenary celebrations Dennis Britain, the surviving member of the original family, personally selected a number of hussars and fusiliers to be included in a two-tier box set, complete with lift-out tray. It was planned for release in 1992, but it did not appear until 1993.

ABOVE **Britains' Green Howards "Grey Box" of drummers and buglers, with escorts and standards. Height: 54mm (2¼in).**

BELOW **The box containing Dennis Britain's personal choice of figures for the company's centenary celebrations. Height: 54mm (2¼in).**

NEW METAL MODELS

Britains' official centenary year was 1993, and three special sets were issued for sale only during that year: there were the Royal Horse Artillery gun team, a Life Guard of 1837 and a Fort Henry Pioneer, these latter two in individual boxes. Limited editions of 4,000 sets of the Royal Regiment of Fusiliers and 5,000 sets of the Band of the Blues and Royals (minus a bandmaster!) were issued, along with red boxes of the 5th Dragoon Guards and the King's Royal Rifle Corps. The William Britain Collectors Club was also started in 1993. In addition to a magazine and membership card, club members receive a special figure each year, which make up into a full band.

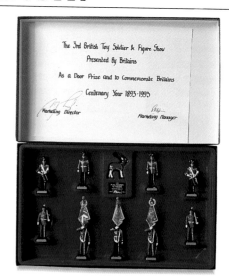

ABOVE **The William Britain limited-edition set of the Royal Regiments of Fusiliers. Height: 54mm (2¼in).**

BELOW **A drum major of the Sherwood Foresters, available only to members of the William Britain Collectors Club. Height: 54mm (2¼in).**

OTHER MATERIALS

Miniature soldiers can be found in all sorts of materials, from ceramic and porcelain to glass, resin, tin, celluloid and even soap. They can vary tremendously in size, but do not really constitute collectable toy soldiers as discussed in this book. Even aluminium, wood and paper soldiers are not a major part of the hobby. However, it is worth mentioning them briefly, as they are not uncommon and can form a pleasing addition to a collection.

This unusual Highlander was made of celluloid, and may be of German origin. Height: 70mm (2¾in).

Krolyn of Copenhagen made this aluminium Robin Hood just prior to World War II. Height: 110mm (4½in).

A tinplate toy soldier made by Louis Marx & Co. of the USA. These figures were designed for use in shooting games along with a pop gun. Height: 50mm (2in).

OTHER MATERIALS

Aluminium is perhaps the material most overlooked by collectors. Most aluminium figures were made in France during the 1930s, by a production process developed by Quiralu. Wend-Al later obtained the Quiralu moulds and produced some aluminium soldiers in the UK in the 1950s, during a period of lead shortage. Such soldiers were described as unbreakable, and they were certainly more resilient than their lead counterparts, but owing to the softer-style casting method they do not carry the same degree of fine detail. Paint tends to chip off them more easily than from other types of toy soldiers, and the bases on the figures are thick, giving them a clumsy appearance.

ABOVE **This aluminium Musketeer was made in France during the mid-1940s, a time of lead shortage. Height: 60mm (2⅜in).**

BELOW **A boxed set of aluminium Toytown figures made by Wend-Al. The contents are based on children dressed in Napoleonic military uniforms, and include a rocking horse, nurse and trees. Height: 54mm (2¼in).**

OTHER MATERIALS

Paper toy soldiers were made in the USA by Parker Bros, Milton Bradley and McLoughlin, usually as part of shooting games in which they formed the targets. Understandably, not many have survived! There are wooden soldiers in existence, but wood has also been an obvious choice for the construction of toy forts. Manufacturers of toy forts often co-operated with their colleagues in the toy-soldier business, to ensure that forts and soldiers would be at the right proportions to each other. Forts can be collectors' items in their own right, and can nicely complement a toy-soldier collection.

ABOVE **This wooden fort was made by Cee Bee around 1952. It was built in three sections so that it folds up into a box. Height: 60cm (2ft.)**

LEFT **This US-made paper soldier probably dates from 1920. Height: 100mm (4in).**

FAR LEFT **Renee North made this flat plywood figure, c. 1971. After North's death figures from this range were sold by Shamus Wade, who runs the Commonwealth Forces History Trust. Height: 100mm (4in).**

TOY SOLDIER SHOWS

Birmingham Model and Toy Soldier Fayre
Held each October. Organizer: David McKenna, 20 Poston Court, Kings Heath, Birmingham B14 5AB, UK.

British Model Soldier Society
National and local branch activities include trade standards. See Societies and Clubs, page 79.

Euro Militaire
A two-day military modelling event held each September at the Leas Cliff Hall, Folkestone, Kent, UK.

Folkestone International Toy Soldier Show
This is held each March at the Metropole Suite, Folkestone, Kent, UK.

Soldiers and Figure Show
Held each February at the Gloucester Leisure Centre. Organizer: Lilliane Tunstill, 110/112 Bath Road, Cheltenham, Gloucestershire, UK.

UK Toy and Model Soldier Show
Organized by *Plastic Warrior* and held each May at the Queen Charlotte Hall, Parkshot, Richmond, Surrey, UK.

Old Toy Soldier Show, Chicago
Held each September at the Hyatt Regency, Woodfield, Schaumburg, Illinois. Organized in conjunction with *Old Toy Soldier* magazine. Contact Don Pielin, 1009 Kenilworth, Wheeling, Illinois, USA.

Toronto Old Soldier Sale
Held each October at the Regal Constellation Hotel, 900 Dixon Road, Toronto, Canada. Organizer: Stewart Saxe.

Annual East Coast Toy Soldier Show and Sale
Held each November at the Fairleigh Dickinson University, Hackensack, New Jersey, USA, and run in conjunction with *Toy Soldier Review* magazine. Contact: Bill Lango.

The Camileri Westchester Toy Soldier Show
Held each November at the Westchester County Centre, White Plains, New York, USA. Contact: Frank Fusco.

West Coaster Toy Soldier Show
Held each March at the Inn at The Park Hotel, 1855 South Harbor Boulevard, Anaheim, California 92802, USA. Contact: Bob Fisher.

MFCA (Miniature Figure Collectors of America) Annual Show and Exhibition
Held each May at Valley Forge Convention Centre, King of Prussia, Pennsylvania, USA. Contact: Alban Shaw.

Hobby Militaire of the Ontario Model Soldier Society
Held each June at the Novotel North York, 3 Park Home Avenue, North York, Toronto, Canada. Contact: Ted Kennedy.

Annapolis Toy Soldier Show
Held each July at the Annapolis Hotel, Annapolis, Maryland, USA. Contact: Dick Sossi.

Indiana Toy Soldier Show
Held each March at the Ramada Inn, 7701 42nd Street, Indianapolis, Indiana, USA. Contact: Barry Carter.

North East Toy Soldier Society Soldier Show
Held each April at Dedham, Massachusetts, USA. Contact: Dick Charlesworth, 121 Cherry Brook Road, Weston, MA 02193, USA.

Long Island Toy Soldier Show
Held each September at Elks Lodge, 57 Hempstead Avenue, Lynbrook, Long Island, New York, USA. Contact: Vinny Pugliese.

Kulmbach Deutschen und Internationale Zinnfiguren Borse Show
Held in August on alternate years at Kulmbach, Bavaria. Details from German Tourist Information.

FURTHER READING

Asquith, Stuart, *The Collector's Guide to New Toy Soldiers,* Argus Books, Hemel Hempstead, 1991

Carman, W. Y., *Model Soldiers,* Charles Letts & Co., London, 1973

Fontana, Dennis, *The War Toys 2: The Story of Lineol,* New Cavendish Books, London, 1991

Garratt, John G., *Model Soldiers: A Collector's Guide,* Seeley Services, London, 1965

Garratt, John G., *Collecting Model Soldiers,* David & Charles, Newton Abbot, 1975

Garratt, John G., *The World Encyclopedia of Model Soldiers,* Frederick Muller, London, 1981

Greenhill, Peter, *Heraldic Miniature Knights,* Guild of Master Craftsmen, 1991

Johnson, Peter, *Toy Armies,* B. T. Batsford, London, 1981

Joplin, Norman, *British Toy Figures 1900–Present,* Arms & Armour Press, London, 1987

Joplin, Norman, *The Great Book of Hollow-cast Figures,* New Cavendish Books, London, 1993

Kearton, George, *The Collector's Guide to Plastic Toy Soldiers,* Ross Anderson Publications, 1987

Kurtz, Henry L. and Ehrlich, Burtt, *The Art of the Toy Soldier,* New Cavendish Books, London, 1979

London Toy and Model Museum, *On Guard* (catalogue of exhibition), New Cavendish Books, London, 1984

McKenzie, Ian, *Collecting Old Toy Soldiers,* B. T. Batsford, London, 1975

Nevins, Edward, *Forces of the British Empire 1914,* Vandamere Press, 1993

O'Brien, Richard, *Collecting Toy Soldiers no. 1,* Books Americana, 1990

O'Brien, Richard, *Collecting Toy Soldiers, no. 2,* Books Americana, 1992

Opie, James, *Britains Toy Soldiers 1893–1932,* Gollancz, London, 1985

Opie, James, *British Toy Soldiers 1893 to the Present,* Arms & Armour Press, 1985

Opie, James, *Phillips Collectors' Guides: Toy Soldiers,* Boxtree, London 1989

Opie, James, *Collecting Toy Soldiers,* New Cavendish Books, London, 1992

Opie, James, *The Great Book of Britains,* New Cavendish Books, London, 1993

Pielin, Don, *American Dimestore Soldiers,* private publication, 1975

Polaine, Reggie and Halkins, David, *The War Toys 1: The Story of Hausser-Elastolin* (2nd edition), New Cavendish Books, London, 1991

Richards, L. W., *Old British Model Soldiers 1893–1918,* Arms & Armour Press, 1970

Roer, Hans H., *Old German Toy Soldiers,* private publication, 1993

Rose, Andrew, *The Collector's All-colour Guide to Toy Soldiers,* Salamander, London, 1985

Wallis, Joe, *Regiments of All Nations,* private publication, 1981

Wallis, Joe, *Armies of the World,* private publication, 1983

PERIODICALS

The following periodicals contain information about, and articles on, toy soldiers and toy soldier collecting.

Les Amis de Starlux
See Societies and Clubs, page 79.

Bulletin
The journal issued by the British Model Soldier Society to members only. See Societies and Clubs, page 79.

Collector's Gazette
A general hobby newspaper, 10 editions each year, including regular features and reports on toy soldier shows and auctions. Contact: 200 Nuncargate Road, Kirby-in-Ashfield, Nottinghamshire NG17 9AG, UK.

Figuren Magazine
The magazine for Germany's toy soldier collectors. Contact: Andreas Pletruschka, Spenerstrasse 17, 1000 Berlin 21, Germany.

Holger Eriksson Collector Society
A quarterly newsletter specializing in the products and associated companies of Eriksson. Contact: Lou Sandbote, 5307E Mockingbird, Suite 802, Dallas, Texas 75206–5109, USA.

Military Hobbies
A bi-monthly magazine, of which a large proportion is devoted to toy soldier manufacturing products. Contact: Pireme Publishing Ltd, 34 Chatsworth Road, Charminster, Bournemouth BH6 8SW, UK.

Military Modelling
Includes a monthly soldier box column giving details of toy soldier products and events. Contact: Argus Specialist

Publications, Argus House, Boundary Way, Hemel Hempstead HP2 7ST, UK.

Old Toy Soldier Newsletter
A bi-monthly publication covering all aspects of old and new toy soldier collecting. Contact: Steve and Josie Sommers (editors), 209 North Lombard, Oak Park, Illinois 60302–2503, USA.

Plastic Figures and Playset Collector
Specializes in plastic figures produced by Marx. Contact: Tom Terry (editor), PO Box 1355, La Crosse, Wisconsin 54602–1355, USA.

The Plastic Warrior
Magazine, available by subscription, for collectors interested in and specializing in collecting plastic toy soldiers. Contact: 65 Walton Court, Woking, Surrey GU21 5EE, UK.

Toy Soldier Review
A quarterly publication covering old and new toy soldiers. Contact: Bill Lango (editor), c/o Vintage Castings, 127 74th Street, North Bergen, New Jersey 07047, USA.

The William Britain
The magazine of the William Britain Collectors Club. See Societies and Clubs, page 79.

Woody's Word
A quarterly newsletter covering toy soldier news and events. Contact: M. D. Paulussen, 19 Seneca Trail, Wayne, New Jersey 07470, USA.

SOCIETIES, CLUBS AND AUCTIONS

Les Amis de Starlux (The Friends of Starlux)
A regular magazine provides details of Starlux's products. Details from: Patrice Reynaud, 9 Grand rue, 11400 Ville Neuve, La Comptar, France.

British Model Soldier Society
This long-established society caters for the needs of the toy and model soldier collector. There are regional branches, exhibitions and competitions and an annual national event in London. Part of the society's own collection is displayed at Hatfield House, Hertfordshire. Membership details from: Ian R. Webb, Honorary Treasurer, 35 St John's Road, Chelmsford, Essex CM2 0TX, UK.

Toy Soldier Collectors of America
A directory of members both in the USA and throughout the world. Details from: John Giddings, 5340 40th Avenue North, St Petersburgh, Florida 33709, USA.

William Britain Collectors Club
Membership includes a special Britains figure, issued each year exclusively to members, who also receive a twice-yearly magazine and details of forthcoming Britains figures. Membership details from: William Britain Collectors Club, PO Box 1946, Halesowen, West Midlands B63 3TS, UK.

AUCTIONS

Christies, South Kensington Ltd.
Contact: Hugo Marsh or Daniel Agnew, 85 Old Brompton Road, London SW7 3LD, UK.

Lacy Scott, 10 Risbygate Street, Bury St Edmunds, Suffolk, UK. Contact: George Beevis or Peter Crichton.

Phillips Bayswater, 10 Salem Road, Bayswater, London W2 4DL, UK. Contact: James Opie (consultant).

Wallis & Wallis, West Street Auction Galleries, Lewes, Sussex BN7 2NJ, UK. Contact: Glen Butler.

Henry Kurtz Ltd, 163 Amsterdam Avenue, Suite 136, New York, NY, USA 10023.

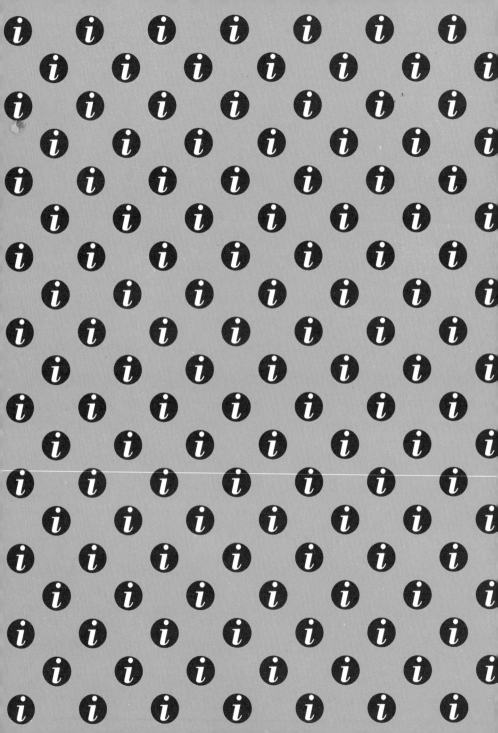